# The Trial

*and*

# King Ubu

**Simon Stephens** began his theatrical career as a tutor in the Young Writers' Programme at the Royal Court Theatre. His plays for theatre include *Bluebird* (Royal Court Theatre, London Upstairs, 1998, directed by Gordon Anderson); *Herons* (Royal Court Theatre Upstairs, 2001); *Port* (Royal Exchange Theatre, Manchester, 2002); *One Minute* (Crucible Theatre, Sheffield, 2003 and Bush Theatre, London, 2004); *Christmas* (Bush Theatre, 2004); *Country Music* (Royal Court Theatre Upstairs, 2004); *On the Shore of the Wide World* (Royal Exchange Theatre and National Theatre, London, 2005); *Motortown* (Royal Court Theatre Downstairs, 2006); *Pornography* (Deutsches Schauspielhaus, Hanover, 2007; Edinburgh Festival/ Birmingham Rep, 2008 and Tricycle Theatre, London, 2009); *Harper Regan* (National Theatre, 2008); *Sea Wall* (Bush Theatre, 2008/Traverse Theatre, Edinburgh, 2009); *Heaven* (Traverse Theatre, 2009); *Punk Rock* (Lyric Hammersmith, London, and Royal Exchange Theatre, 2009); *The Trial of Ubu* (Essen Schauspielhaus/Toneelgroep Amsterdam, 2010); *A Thousand Stars Explode in the Sky* (co-written with David Eldridge and Robert Holman; Lyric Hammersmith, London, 2010); *Marine Parade* (co-written with Mark Eitzel; Brighton International Festival, 2010); *T5* (Traverse Theatre, 2010); and *Wastwater* (Royal Court Theatre Downstairs, 2011). His radio plays include *Five Letters Home to Elizabeth* (BBC Radio 4, 2001) and *Digging* (BBC Radio 4, 2003). His screenwriting includes the two-part serial *Dive* (with Dominic Savage) for Granada/BBC (2009) and a short film adaptation of *Pornography* for Channel 4's 'Coming Up' series (2009). Awards include the Pearson Award for Best New Play, 2001, the Olivier Award for Best New Play for *On the Shore of the Wide World*, 2005; and *Theater Heute*'s for *Motortown* (2007), *Pornography* (2008) and *Wastwater* (2011) for Best Foreign Play.

Simon Stephens

# The Trial of Ubu
*and*
# King Ubu

Methuen Drama

**Published by Methuen Drama 2012**

Methuen Drama, an imprint of Bloomsbury Publishing Plc

1 3 5 7 9 10 8 6 4 2

Methuen Drama
Bloomsbury Publishing Plc
50 Bedford Square
London WC1B 3DP
www.methuendrama.com

First published by Methuen Drama in 2012

ISBN: 978 1 408 17243 8

A CIP catalogue record for this book is available from the British Library

Available in the USA from Bloomsbury Academic & Professional, 175 Fifth
Avenue/3rd Floor, New York, NY 10010. www.BloomsburyAcademicUSA.com

Typeset by Mark Heslington Ltd, Scarborough, North Yorkshire
Printed and bound in Great Britain by CPI Group (UK) Ltd, Croydon CR0 4YY

# Contents

# The Trial of Ubu

*The Trial of Ubu* premiered, with *Ubu Roi*, at the Schauspielhaus Essen in a co-production with the Toneelgroep Amsterdam on 16 April 2010. It transferred to Toneelgroep Amsterdam on 1 May 2010, and featured the following cast and creative team:

| | |
|---|---|
| Roeland Fernhout | Roland Riebeling |
| Nicola Mastroberadino | Dimitrij Schaad |
| Hadewych Minis | Werner Strenger |
| Frieda Pittoors | Leon Voorberg |
| Alwin Pulincks | Judith van der Werff |

*Director*   Sebastian Nübling
*Designer*   Muriel Gerstner
*Music*   Lars Wittershagen
*Dramaturgs*   Corien Baart and Thomas Laue.


*The Trial of Ubu* opened at the Hampstead Theatre on 18 January 2012, and featured the following cast and creative team:

| | |
|---|---|
| Nikki Amuka-Bird | Paul McCleary |
| Josie Daxter | Rob Ostlere |
| Kate Duchêne | George Taylor |

*Director*   Katie Mitchell
*Designer*   Lizzie Clachan
*Lighting Designer*   Lucy Carter
*Composer*   Paul Clark
*Sound Designer*   Tom Hackley
*Movement*   Joseph Alford

## Characters

**Voice of Prince Billiam**
**Registrar**
**Judge**
**Ubu**
**Defence**
**Prosecution**
**Achras**
**Norbert Nurdle**
**McClub**
**Ma Ubu**
**Jailor**
**Major General-in-Chief**

*This play should be performed immediately after a performance of*
Ubu Roi *by Alfred Jarry or combinations of his* Ubu *plays.*

*The play is set in Trial Room 2 of The Hague and surrounding rooms.*

*It is set in the present day.*

*Scenes which are consecutive to one another but which take place in different locations should run straight into one another without apparent pause or scene change. The location is only prescribed so as to suggest a change in energy.*

*A sudden, total blackout.*

*Noise.*

*Through the noise we hear a distorted voice. It is the voice of* **Prince Billiam**, *the adult child of King Wenceslas. The noise gets louder throughout until it almost drowns the voice.*

**Prince Billiam**     When you destroy structure you leave not liberty but chaos.

When you destroy structure you leave not joy but despair. When you destroy simplicity and structure you leave not equality but greed and tyranny and horror and fear. This cannot and will not be endured. You cannot get away with this.

We have tolerated that which cannot be tolerated for too long. We have endured that which is unendurable. We have behaved with grace and with dignity at times of fear and horror and outrage. The time has come for us to endure no longer. The time has come for us to fear no more. Let it be known that when Ubu talks of liberty he means obesity and flatulence and violence and greed. When Ubu talks of democracy he means dictatorship. When Ubu talks of freedom he means fear and destruction. He is a man steeped in blood. He is a man boned in horror. He is schooled in violence and in shit and in revelry.

He has built our country, no, let me say that he has built *your* country upon his own wealth and his tyranny and his savagery. He is a thief. He is a murderer. He can steal no more. He can kill no more.

*Noise crescendos and stops suddenly.*

*The courtroom is revealed.*

**Ubu**, **Judge**, **Defence**, **Prosecution**, **Registrar**.

*The* **Judge** *and counsel are dressed and prepared for the session.*

*In the courtroom multiple translations are used. Words are translated into German, Dutch, English and French where appropriate.*

*Where appropriate we can hear the translation.*

*Where appropriate the multiple translation becomes cacophonous.*

*Sometimes there may be discrepancies between the spoken statements and their translations.*

*Sometimes the translation is on a soundtrack that slows down or speeds up unnaturally.*

*Sometimes the sound drops out altogether.*

**Registrar**   The International Tribunal into the Former Kingdom of Baleshnik is now in session. All rise for the President Judge.

*All stand. The* **Judge** *examines the courtroom. Sits.*

**Judge**   Thank you. Thank you ladies and gentlemen. Please be seated.

*The rest of the court sits.* **Ubu** *sits.*

*The* **Judge** *writes something at length. He examines the courtroom. He examines* **Ubu**.

**Judge**   Registrar. Please read the indictment. Thank you.

*The* **Judge** *continues to write. The* **Registrar** *stands. He reads from a document.*

**Registrar**   The Special Court for the Former Kingdom of Baleshnik Case No. SCFKB–2009–01–PU.

The Prosecutor against Pa Ubu also known as Father Ubu also known as Konig Ubu also known as Ubu Roi also known as Pere Ubu also known as Ubu Rex.

SECOND AMENDED INDICTMENT
The Prosecutor for the Special Court for the Former Kingdom of Baleshnik under Article 12 of the Statute of

the Special Court for the Former Kingdom of Baleshnik (hereafter referred to as 'the Statute') charges Pa Ubu also known as Father Ubu also known as Konig Ubu also known as Ubu Roi also known as Pere Ubu also known as Ubu Rex with CRIMES AGAINST HUMANITY, violations of Article 3 common to the Geneva Conventions and of additional Protocol 2 and of other serious violations of international humanitarian law, in violation of Articles 2, 3 and 4 of the Statute as set forth below.

THE ACCUSED
Pa Ubu also known as Father Ubu also known as Konig Ubu also known as Ubu Roi also known as Pere Ubu also known as Ubu Rex was born on 8 September 1873 at Saint Brieuc in France.

From a date unspecified the ACCUSED held the office of King of the Former Kingdom of Baleshnik, herein after known as the FKB. This tenure afforded with it the position of Commander-in-Chief of the Kingdom of Baleshnik's Military, the KBM. This was an office held until he was deposed after the Russian invasion of Baleshnik in 1913. He was arrested in Frankfurt am Main on 12 March 2008.

CHARGES
By acts or omissions in relation to the below described events, the ACCUSED, pursuant to Article 6.1 and, or alternatively, Article 6.3 of the Statute, is individually criminally responsible for the crimes alleged below:

TERRORISING THE CIVILIAN POPULATION
Count 1: Acts of Terrorism, a VIOLATION OF ARTICLE 3 COMMON TO THE GENEVA CONVENTIONS AND OF ADDITIONAL PROTOCOL 2, punishable under Article 3.d of the Statute.

UNLAWFUL KILLINGS
Count 2: Murder, a CRIME AGAINST HUMANITY punishable under Article 2.a of the Statute.

In addition or in the alternative:

Count 3: Violence to life, health and physical or
mental well-being of persons, in particular murder, a
VIOLATION OF ARTICLE 3 COMMON TO THE
GENEVA CONVENTIONS AND OF ADDITIONAL
PROTOCOL 2, punishable under Article 3.a of the
Statute.

PHYSICAL VIOLENCE
Count 4; Violence to life, health and physical or mental
well-being of persons, in particular cruel treatment, a
VIOLATION OF ARTICLE 3 COMMON TO THE
GENEVA CONVENTIONS AND OF ADDITIONAL
PROTOCOL 2, punishable under Article 3.a of the
Statute.

In addition, or in the alternative:

Count 5: Other inhumane acts, a CRIME AGAINST
HUMANITY, punishable under Article 2.i of the Statute.

ABDUCTIONS AND FORCED LABOUR
Count 6: Enslavement, a CRIME AGAINST
HUMANITY, punishable under Article 2.c of the Statute.

LOOTING
Count 7: Pillage, a VIOLATION OF ARTICLE 3
COMMON TO THE GENEVA CONVENTIONS AND
OF PROTOCOL 2, punishable under Article 3.f of the
Statute.

USE OF CHILD SOLDIERS
Count 8: Conscripting or enlisting children under the
age of 15 years into armed forces or groups or using
them to participate actively in hostilities, a SERIOUS
VIOLATION OF INTERNATIONAL HUMANITARIAN
LAW, punishable under Article 4.c of the Statute.

INDIVIDUAL CRIMINAL RESONSIBILITY
The ACCUSED by his acts or omissions is individually
criminally responsible pursuant to Article 6.1 of the

Statute for the crimes referred to in Articles 2, 3 and 4 of the Statute as alleged in this amended indictment, which crimes the ACCUSED planned, instigated, ordered and committed, or in whose planning, preparation or execution the ACCUSED otherwise aided and abetted, or which crimes amounted to or were involved within a common plan, design or purpose in which the ACCUSED participated, or were a reasonably foreseeable consequence of such common plan, design or purpose.

In addition, or alternatively, pursuant to Article 6.3 of the Statute the ACCUSED, while holding positions of superior responsibility and exercising command and control over subordinate members of the FKB and KBM, is individually responsible for the crimes referred to in Articles 2, 3 and 4 of the Statute as alleged in this amended indictment. The ACCUSED is responsible for the criminal act of his subordinates in that he knew or had reason to know that the subordinate was about to commit such acts or had done so and the ACCUSED failed to take the necessary and reasonable measures to prevent such acts or to punish the perpetrators thereof.

Thank you Your Honour.

*The* **Registrar** *sits. The* **Judge** *makes more notes. He turns to* **Ubu**.

**Judge**    Mr Ubu could you stand please.

**Ubu** *stands*.

**Judge**    Mr Ubu can you confirm to the court that you speak English.

**Ubu**    I can Your Honour. I do.

**Judge**    Mr Ubu do you understand French?

**Ubu**    Yes.

**Judge**    Mr Ubu do you understand German?

**Ubu**    Yes.

**Judge**   Do you understand Russian?

**Ubu**   Yes.

**Judge**   Mr Ubu did you hear the charges levelled against you in the indictment read to you.

**Ubu**   I did Your Honour.

**Judge**   Mr Ubu did you understand those charges?

**Ubu**   I would like to make it clear to the court that I remain the King of the Kingdom of Baleshnik and the Commander-in-Chief of the Military of the Kingdom of Baleshnik.

*A pause.*

**Judge**   I'm sorry Mr Ubu, I don't know whether you heard my question. Mr Ubu I'm simply asking whether you understand the charges brought against you in the indictment. Can you hear what I am saying to you Mr Ubu? The indictment which has just been read out do you understand the charges that have been brought against you?

**Ubu**   Yes Your Honour. I do.

**Judge**   Now I'm going to give you the chance to answer those charges by entering a plea of either guilty or not guilty. I'll go through each of the counts one by one and perhaps if you would be good enough to tell me whether you plead guilty or not guilty. The first count is count number one – terrorising the civilian population, namely acts of terrorism – how do you plead to that Mr Ubu? Guilty or not guilty?

**Ubu**   Your Honour there are some issues I don't understand. These are issues not about the charges but rather, if it pleases Your Honour, about this court and its right to exercise jurisdiction over me, as the King of the Kingdom of Baleshnik.

*A brief pause.*

**Judge**   Mr Ubu I don't know what advice you've been given –

**Ubu**   Why wasn't I tried in the International Criminal Court?

*A brief pause.*

**Judge**   Mr Ubu. Counsel. I have decided for the sake of clarification and to render such interruption as this further unnecessary to address your query as quickly and as finally as possible.

**Defence**   Thank you Your Honour. I apologise for the interruption on my client's behalf.

**Judge**   The nature of the crimes for which you are being tried –

**Ubu**   I have committed no crimes.

**Judge**   The nature of the crimes for which you are being tried renders them outside the jurisdiction of the International Criminal Court, which has no jurisdiction to investigate crimes of aggression.

**Ubu**   I repeat I have committed no crimes.

**Judge**   Mr Ubu, don't interrupt me.

*A pause.*

**Defence**   I'm sorry Your Honour. I apologise for the interruption on my client's behalf.

**Judge**   The nature of the crimes for which you are being tried also falls outside the jurisdiction of the International Criminal Court because of the temporal limitations of that court. Mr Ubu may I remind you that you accepted the right to raise all these issues in the pre-trial chamber.

**Ubu**   Did I?

**Judge**   They were raised there.

**Ubu**   Were they?

**Judge**   They were overruled there

**Ubu**   I don't remember that happening.

**Judge**   Now unless there are further questions pertaining to new inquiries –

**Ubu**   When did that happen?

**Judge**   Unless there are further questions pertaining to new inquiries can we return Mr Ubu to the issue of the plea?

**Ubu**   Is that why you had to call this Statute in the first place? Because this court falls outside all recognised international jurisdiction you had to invent new jurisdiction.

**Judge**   Can we return Mr Ubu please to the issue of your plea?

**Ubu**   There is no justice here.

**Judge**   Mr Ubu it is not an issue of this court's to establish justice but to implement law.

**Ubu**   This is a political court. You are politicians. I refute the legality of this court.

**Judge**   Mr Ubu should you refuse to enter a plea then according to Article 12 of the Independent Criminal Tribunal for the Former Kingdom of Baleshnik an automatic plea of not guilty will be entered on your behalf.

**Ubu**   I think there is something in the notion of punishment that you imagine cleanses you. It's not true. It's just how you feel. You're trying to take something that's inside you and put it in an institution. It won't work.

*

*Courtroom.*

*Opening statement.*

*The case for the Prosecution.*

**Prosecution**, **Defence**, **Judge**, **Achras**, **Registrar**, **Ubu**.

**Prosecution**   Could you identify yourself to the Court?

**Achras**   My name is Achras.

**Prosecution**   And Mr Achras you are a forensics analyst at the University of the Former Kingdom of Baleshnik is that correct?

**Achras**   That's correct.

**Prosecution**   Mr Achras I'm correct in thinking that you compiled a forensics analysis of the mass grave found on the peripheries of the Royal Castle in the capital of Baleshnik is that correct?

**Achras**   That's correct. Yes.

**Prosecution**   Mr Achras could you identify on the architectural ground plan of the Royal Castle whereabouts the grave was found?

**Achras**   It was found in cellars underneath the grounds to the south-east of the Castle. Here.

**Prosecution**   Mr Achras on initial investigation how many bodies were found to be held in these graves?

**Achras**   It was believed on initial estimate that upwards of 800 bodies were found there.

**Prosecution**   Mr Achras the report you published suggests that that figure is inaccurate is that correct?

**Achras**   It is correct. I took a team of analysts down there on seven different occasions. We concluded that a more accurate figure would be something in the region of 1600 bodies.

**Prosecution**    Mr Achras according to your findings how did these people die?

**Achras**    We carried out investigations on thirty-seven bodies in the grave. Seven of these bodies appear to have died from the impact of the fall. There is a forty-seven feet fall from the door of the cellar to the cellar floor. As more bodies built up on the floor of the cellar though clearly the landing was softened and the distance shortened. We found twenty-four bodies died from suffocation.

**Prosecution**    Twenty-four of your thirty-seven bodies investigated. Roughly two-thirds.

**Achras**    That's right.

**Prosecution**    Two-thirds of 1600 is over a thousand isn't it?

**Achras**    It is. One thousand and sixty-six I think.

**Prosecution**    One thousand and sixty-six people died from suffocation in a mass grave within a hundred yards of the palace of the King.

**Defence**    Objection Your Honour. This is pure speculation.

**Judge**    Upheld. Will prosecution counsel please concern himself only with asking questions of his witnesses? Please remove Prosecution's previous comments from the record.

**Prosecution**    The remaining six bodies, how did they die?

**Achras**    There is evidence that the remaining six bodies we investigated died from strangulation rather than suffocation and that a short period after their death there is evidence to suggest that, in some way, their flesh was gnawed at.

**Prosecution**    Gnawed at? By rats?

**Achras**    The evidence from the size and particular nature of the bite marks would suggest not. It would suggest rather that they were human bite marks.

**Prosecution**    They had human bite marks in their flesh? What would have caused that?

**Achras**    It's difficult to say for certain. Although the most probable explanation is that other people started biting them.

**Prosecution**    Why on earth would they have done that?

**Achras**    Investigation of the stomach contents of two of the twenty-four bodies which died from suffocation shows evidence of the presence of uncooked flesh. Further analysis of this flesh revealed it to be is consistent in texture and density with uncooked human flesh.

**Prosecution**    Are you suggesting that people started eating one another in the grave?

**Achras**    I would say that was the case.

**Defence**    Objection Your Honour this is entirely irrelevant. It has a macabre fascination but teaches us nothing of the charges brought against my client.

**Judge**    Objection upheld. Prosecution will, please, stick to the task in hand. Registrar please remove relevant comments from the record.

**Prosecution**    Mr Achras, were you able to carry out inspections on the door to the cellar.

**Achras**    We investigated DNA and fingerprinting evidence on the door.

**Prosecution**    And what did your investigations reveal?

**Achras**    That as far as we can tell only one person ever came into contact with that door.

**Prosecution**    And is there any way of identifying who that person may have been?

**Achras**    It was Mr Ubu.

**Prosecution**    No further questions Your Honour.

**Defence**   Mr Achras when did you become President of the Campaign for Justice in Baleshnik?

**Prosecution**   Objection your honour! I fail to see the relevance of this line of questioning.

**Judge**   Overruled. Please continue. Please answer the question Mr Achras.

**Achras**   Three years ago.

**Defence**   Could you describe to me what the Campaign for Justice in Baleshnik campaigns for?

**Achras**   The rights to freedom of speech and movement within the FKB. Right to free trial.

**Defence**   In your opinion what is the major cause preventing these freedoms?

**Achras**   There are many causes.

**Defence**   The main cause.

**Achras**   In my opinion the reign of Mr Ubu was particularly destructive.

**Defence**   You campaigned to see him convicted didn't you Mr Achras?

**Achras**   I campaigned to see him tried.

**Defence**   In an interview with *News Day* on 24 January 2008 you are quoted as saying that 'Ubu is an animal. He behaves as though his conscience has been cut away from him, stuffed into a box and shoved into a sewer.' Did you say that Mr Achras?

**Achras**   I don't remember saying those exact words.

**Defence**   Do you recognise the sentiment?

**Achras**   I, er, yes I do recognise it as a sentiment.

**Defence**   Mr Achras, Mr Ubu moved into your house in May 1913, did he not?

**Achras**  He did. Yes.

**Defence**  Did you invite him into your home or did he occupy it by force?

**Achras**  He occupied it by force.

**Defence**  How did he treat you while he was a guest in your house?

**Achras**  I don't know what you mean.

**Defence**  Is it not true, Mr Achras, that while he was a guest in your house he subjected you to ritualistic and continued acts of humiliation?

**Achras**  There was occasion when –

**Defence**  Did he assault you? Did he assault you Mr Achras? Did he assault you or didn't he?

**Achras**  He did.

**Defence**  And it is this assault that motivated your decision to come and act as a witness in his prosecution isn't it, Mr Achras?

**Achras**  No. It absolutely isn't.

**Defence**  You're called Mr Achras as an impartial witness. You are in no way impartial are you Mr Achras?

\*

*Courtroom*

*Case for the Prosecution.*

**Prosecution**, **Defence**, **Judge**, **Norbert Nurdle**, **Registrar**, **Ubu**.

**Norbert Nurdle**  There was a noise outside my house. I can hear a voice. 'Open up! Fucking open up in there!' I open the door. He comes in. He asks 'Who is the oldest?' I tell him I am. He threatened to hurt me. He threatened to get his friends to attack me. He said they'd cut off my fingers. He said he wants my tax. I tell him I'd already paid the taxes I owed. And he goes 'I've changed the rules.' He tells me everybody has to pay the tax twice. I remember he said 'Simple innit? I make my fortune, kill the whole world and bugger off.' I asked him for pity. He refused to let me off. I was so angry. I tried to charge him. But he was too strong. He killed my wife and my son and my friend. I ran away before he could catch me.

**Prosecution**   Mr Nurdle, when Mr Ubu talked about changing the rules did he say 'The rules have changed'?

**Norbert Nurdle**   No. He goes 'I've changed the rules.'

**Prosecution**   Thank you. And Mr Nurdle when you talk about what he said before the fight you claim he said 'Simple innit? I make my fortune, kill the whole world and bugger off.' Are you paraphrasing or is that a quote? Are they the exact words he said?

**Norbert Nurdle**   The exact words. They stuck in my head.

**Achras**   No further questions Your Honour.

**Defence**   How old are you Mr Nurdle?

**Norbert Nurdle**   I'm 183 years old.

**Defence**   Who exactly was it that killed your wife Mr Nurdle?

**Norbert Nurdle**   It was one of Ubu's soldiers but he gave the order.

**Defence**   Which soldier was it Mr Nurdle?

**Norbert Nurdle**   The one with brown hair. There was one of the soldiers and he had brown hair.

**Defence**   And how tall was he?

**Norbert Nurdle**   Six foot. Maybe five foot ten. Maybe a bit taller. Six foot two.

**Defence**   So anywhere between five foot ten, maybe, and six foot two? What was his name Mr Nurdle?

**Norbert Nurdle**   I didn't hear his name.

**Defence**   You didn't hear it?

**Norbert Nurdle**   No. I, I think it was Dog Dog. Pile Dog. Pog Dog. Something like that.

**Defence**   You think?

**Norbert Nurdle**   It might have, it was ninety-eight years ago.

**Defence**   Is it something you don't think about very much?

**Norbert Nurdle**   I think about it every day.

**Defence**   It must have been very upsetting to watch your best friend killed and your wife and your son, was it?

**Norbert Nurdle**   It was horrible.

**Defence**   What did you do?

**Norbert Nurdle**   What did I do?

**Defence**   After they were killed? Did you try and help them? Did you stay with their bodies?

Mr Nurdle will you answer the question? What did you do after their death?

**Norbert Nurdle**   I left.

**Defence**   I'm sorry I didn't hear that could you repeat your answer please?

**Norbert Nurdle**   I left.

**Defence**   You left?

**Norbert Nurdle**   –

**Defence**   You ran away?

**Norbert Nurdle**   –

**Defence**   I imagine the guilt from what you have done is awful, is it?

**Prosecution**   Objection Your Honour. This questioning is ill-focused.

**Judge**   Overruled.

**Defence**   You shouldn't testify today should you, Mr Nurdle? Because it's impossible for you to testify with clarity on the events of that night because a combination of guilt and trauma has rendered you mentally ill.

**Prosecution**   Objection, Your Honour, surely Mr Nurdle exemplifies exactly the kind of people who must testify. To build a judicial infrastructure that excludes the possibility of an emotional human response to a crime is to create something arid and inert and pointless.

**Defence**   Counter-objection, Your Honour, it is only through this exclusion that the Court is able to establish any kind of clarity.

**Judge**   Objection overruled. Counter-objection sustained.

**Defence**   No further questions, Your Honour.

**Judge**   Thank you counsel. Thank you Mr Nurdle. Counsel, ladies and gentlemen. That concludes our proceedings for today. We'll adjourn now and re-convene at 9.30 on Monday morning.

\*

*Courtroom.*

*Case for the Prosecution.*

**Prosecution**, **Defence**, **Judge**, **McClub**, **Registrar**, **Ubu**.

**McClub**  The plan was that he was going to stamp on the King's foot. And when the King got angry he would shout 'shit'. And that was our cue.

**Prosecution**  To kill the King?

**McClub**  To kill the King and take his crown and give it to him.

**Prosecution**  When did you first hear about this plan?

**McClub**  A week earlier. He spoke to the Major General-in-Chief about it at dinner. And actually he was a bit. He went a bit mad.

**Prosecution**  Mr McClub you hated Wenceslas didn't you?

**McClub**  I did. Yes.

**Prosecution**  You wanted him to be killed didn't you?

**McClub**  I didn't mind about that.

**Prosecution**  It was your idea wasn't it? You and the Major General-in-Chief?

**McClub**  No. No. It wasn't. We were surprised when Ubu suggested it. 'Cause he was always a bit of a coward. We went along with it but it was his idea.

**Prosecution**  After the King was killed what happened?

**McClub**  We gave the crown to Ubu and he ordered us to kill everybody else.

**Prosecution**  He ordered you?

**McClub**  He was the King.

**Prosecution**  Who exactly did he order you to kill?

**McClub**  The Prince. Other people in the crowd.

**Prosecution**  What do you think would have happened if you'd refused?

**McClub**  He would have killed us. He told us.

**Prosecution**   How old were you at the time?

**McClub**   I was fourteen.

**Prosecution**   You were present at the Christmas massacre of 1913 weren't you?

**McClub**   Yes. I was. Yes.

**Prosecution**   Could you describe what you remember?

**McClub**   Well Ubu got all the bankers together and the judges and the snobs, the, er –

**Prosecution**   The aristocracy.

**McClub**   That's right the aristocracy. And he says that by 'royal decree' he's going to kill all the gentry and steal the land. And he had a chute above a cellar.

**Prosecution**   Where was this? Could you show us on the plan? For the purposes of the Court could it be recorded that Mr McClub is pointing to the area identified by Mr Achras as the mass grave established after the massacre?

**McClub**   He opened the door to the cellar. They fell in. The noise they made was awful. And Ma Ubu was saying 'Don't do it. Don't do it. You've gone too far.' And so was the Major General-in-Chief and the boys were a bit freaked out because there were fucking, sorry, there were hundreds of these people. And he did it to the judges because he wanted their power he said. And he asked the bankers for all their money and they said no so he did the same to them.

**Prosecution**   How many people would you guess approximately did Mr Ubu kill on this occasion?

**McClub**   Hundreds and hundreds and hundreds.

**Prosecution**   And how did he seem to feel?

**McClub**   He seemed to think it was funny because he was laughing.

**Prosecution**    That it was funny? The mass execution of over fifteen hundred people?

**McClub**    He seemed to be laughing a lot yes. He always used to watch people getting hurt. That used to make him laugh. And then he was very pleased about all the money he was going to get.

**Prosecution**    Would you describe Mr Ubu as being very concerned with money?

**McClub**    He was mad about it. He talked all the time about how he was going to get more and what he was going to do to get it.

**Prosecution**    Mr McClub why didn't you leave his service?

**McClub**    Well after the Major General-in-Chief left he took us over.

**Prosecution**    What do you mean he took you over?

**McClub**    We were his then.

**Prosecution**    He owned you?

**McClub**    Yeah.

**Prosecution**    Like a slave?

**McClub**    I don't know about that.

**Prosecution**    Did he pay you?

**McClub**    No he didn't.

**Prosecution**    Did he make you work for him?

**McClub**    Yes. All the time. From morning till night. We did labour for him. We did do some killings. We tortured Achras for him. We put him on a stake up his arse. 'Cause he told us to.

**Prosecution**    If you'd refused to do these things what would he have done?

**McClub**   He killed people who refused to work for him.

**Prosecution**   No further questions, Your Honour.

**Defence**   Mr McClub, who gave the order 'Pile on lads' in reference to the killing of King Wenceslas? Was it Mr Ubu or the Major General-in-Chief?

**McClub**   Mr Ubu gave the signal.

**Defence**   Who gave the order? Who said 'Pile on lads'?

**McClub**   That was the Major General-in-Chief.

**Defence**   You worked for him at the time didn't you?

**McClub**   At that time I did. Yes.

**Defence**   Of all the people working for the Major General-in-Chief on that day which one of you actually killed King Wenceslas, Mr McClub?

He was killed by being stabbed under his ribcage. Who stabbed under his ribcage Mr McClub?

Can you answer the question please Mr McClub?

**McClub**   I did.

**Defence**   Thank you. How many people have you killed in your life Mr McClub?

**McClub**   I don't know exactly how many people.

**Defence**   Just so I'm clear in my mind was it more than ten?

**McClub**   Yes it was.

**Defence**   More than twenty?

**McClub**   Yes.

**Defence**   More than fifty?

**McClub**   I think it was about a hundred.

**Defence**   Just so I can be clear in my head Mr McClub, you've killed, yourself, about a hundred people, Mr McClub is that right?

**McClub**   Yes.

**Defence**   What's the youngest person you've killed?

**McClub**   I killed children. The Major General-in-Chief and Mr Ubu told me to kill children.

**Defence**   What age were these children you killed?

**McClub**   About four. Maybe five.

**Defence**   Just so I can be clear in my head Mr McClub how does somebody kill a four-year-old child?

**McClub**   I stabbed them mainly. Sometimes hit them until their heads cracked in a bit.

**Defence**   With your fists?

**McClub**   Or metal. Bits of wood.

**Defence**   Thank you Your Honour I have no further questions.

**Judge**   Mr McClub thank you for coming here today. Thank you for answering these questions with such honesty. You may now leave the Court. You are free to go.

**McClub** *leaves. It takes him a while to take off his headphones and turn off his microphone. The Court watches him leave.*

**Ubu** *begins to rock.*

**Prosecution**   Prosecution calls Ma Ubu.

*There is some time.*

*A woman comes and takes the stand.*

*She doesn't look at* **Ubu**.

**Prosecution**   Could you tell the Court your name please?

**Ma Ubu**   Ma Ubu.

**Prosecution**   Could you tell the Court your relationship to the accused please?

**Ma Ubu**   I'm his wife.

**Prosecution**   Ma Ubu whose idea was it originally to kill King Wenceslas and claim the crown of the FKB?

**Ma Ubu**   It was my idea.

**Prosecution**   Ma Ubu, can you tell the Court, how did Mr Ubu respond to the idea?

**Ma Ubu**   He was very nervous about it. Then I teased him that he wasn't a proper man and he changed his mind and decided to do it.

**Prosecution**   Largely because you mocked him, Ma Ubu, is that right?

**Ma Ubu**   Yes that's right.

**Prosecution**   Ma Ubu, why did you want to become Queen?

**Ma Ubu**   For the money and the clothes mainly.

**Prosecution**   And why did Mr Ubu initially refuse to join you?

**Ma Ubu**   Because he said he was a loyal soldier. It would have been wrong. He should have looked after the King not killed him. At one point he was going to tell the King about my plan and get a reward.

**Prosecution**   But you persuaded him to change his mind.

**Ma Ubu**   I did, yes. Mainly by teasing him.

**Prosecution**   Who planned the details of the killing?

**Ma Ubu**   That was the Major General-in-Chief. And then Mr Ubu refined his idea. And I finished it off.

**Prosecution**   And who gave the final signal for the killing to start?

**Ma Ubu**   Pa Ubu.

**Prosecution**   Ma Ubu after you became King and Queen of the FKB did Mr Ubu change at all?

**Ma Ubu**   Completely.

**Prosecution**   I'm sorry?

**Ma Ubu**   He changed completely.

**Prosecution**   In what way?

**Ma Ubu**   He became obsessed with the money and the power. He wanted to control the law. He wanted to control the banks. He wanted all the land. So he planned to execute the landed gentry, the bankers and the judges of the country.

**Prosecution**   Ma Ubu that wasn't him at all was it? That was you.

**Ma Ubu**   No.

**Prosecution**   You wanted to control the law didn't you Ma Ubu?

**Ma Ubu**   No.

**Prosecution**   You wanted to seize the land from the landed gentry?

**Ma Ubu**   No I didn't.

**Prosecution**   You wanted to control the banks didn't you Ma Ubu?

**Ma Ubu**   No I didn't.

**Prosecution**   And it was your idea to kill the aristocracy and to kill the judges and kill the bankers afterwards wasn't it Ma Ubu?

**Ma Ubu**   No. No it absolutely wasn't. It was all Pa. I warned him against it. I told him not to do it. Even after he'd started. On the actual day of the massacre. I told him he was being cruel and mean and he kept going and was laughing. I told him what would happen.

**Prosecution**    You told him what would happen?

**Ma Ubu**    Yes. I told him that everybody he threw into the cellar would die and that would be bad and people would be angry.

**Prosecution**    You explained the consequences of his actions to him?

**Ma Ubu**    I did yes.

**Prosecution**    Did he hear your explanation?

**Ma Ubu**    Yes.

**Prosecution**    How do you know he heard you?

**Ma Ubu**    Because he said he didn't care. He was King. It was his money anyway. He could do what he wanted.

**Prosecution**    How did that make you feel?

**Ma Ubu**    It was awful because before I did love him. But if anybody tried to stop him he killed them. I tried to stop him once and he tried to kill me. He took people's land. He tortured for fun.

**Prosecution**    He seemed, as you describe it to believe that because he was King he could do what he wanted, would you say that's right?

**Ma Ubu**    He said it was 'by Royal Decree'. He said to me 'I'm not Mr Ubu anymore, Ma. I'm King Ubu now.'

**Prosecution**    No further questions, Your Honour.

**Defence**    How long into your marriage with Mr Ubu did you begin a sexual relationship with the Major General-in-Chief?

**Prosecution**    Objection Your Honour.

**Judge**    Counsel please ensure the relevance of these questions.

**Defence**    Your Honour the questions are relevant because the witness is lying. She wants to falsely incriminate her cuckolded husband and liberate her lover. Don't you Mrs Ubu? How long into your marriage wth Mr Ubu did you begin a sexual relationship with the Major General-in-Chief?

**Ubu**    Hello Ma.

**Judge**    Order.

**Ubu**    It's been a long time. You look a bit different from what you used to look like. You don't look as ugly as you used to look. I do have conjugal rights by the way if you want to have sex.

**Judge**    Order in Court.

**Ubu**    They'll send me to jail for ever now, after what you just said.

**Judge**    Counsel please bring your client under order or I shall be forced to have him removed from the court.

**Ubu** (*shouting*)    She should be here. Not me. She should be here. Not me. She should be here. Not me. She should be here. Not me.

**Judge**    Security.

*The* **Jailor** *enters and tries to contain* **Ubu**. *There is a brief struggle that* **Ubu** *loses.*

**Ubu**    She should be here. Not me. I'm the King. She should be having her head cut off for lying. She should be having her teeth taken out with a hammer. Would you like to watch me take her teeth out with a hammer? Would you like to watch me cut her head off with a knife? It's what she deserves. Do you think I fucking won't? Do you think one day I won't get out of here and cut off her head and her hands and take out her teeth with a hammer? She's a liar. She's dead.

*

*Room off the Court.*

**Defence**, **Prosecution**.

*They are chain-smoking cigarettes.*

**Defence**   The simplicity of the structure is its beauty.

**Prosecution**   I don't know if I believe that any more.

**Defence**   Parliaments decide the law. The courts examine those people accused of contravening that law. And decide how to act accordingly. You don't need to overhaul it. You don't need to re-invent it. You don't need to repair it. It's a system that cuts to the quick of every social organisation we've ever known and it works.

**Prosecution**   It's too simple. It's like we're trying to get out of accepting any blame.

**Defence**   Because we're not to blame.

**Prosecution**   Because there's no means of accommodating context this institution fails. Behaviour is triggered by behaviour. Which is affected by time and by place and by history and geography and the weather and the things that people hear and they smell and they taste and they feel and they see. And we don't judge any of that. We just draw a line and say 'No. This is the action we're going to judge. All we'll ask is did this person do this thing, at this time.'

It's limited. It's historically skewed. Its parameters of judgment are limited in terms of time and space to specifically exculpate any individual or nation involved in the establishment and management of the Court. And those people are not necessarily worthy of exculpation. The things we've done! How dare we judge anybody.'

**Defence**   How dare we not?

**Prosecution**   A judicial institution that lets a self-confessed child murderer walk free and thanks him for his time fails. We fail.

**Defence**   But that doesn't mean we stop trying.

**Prosecution**    Why not?

**Defence**    Because to stop trying in the face of the atrocities carried out by the likes of Ubu is unthinkable.

**Prosecution**    Well maybe the only thing we're really obliged to do, as sentient human beings, is think the unthinkable.

Let me ask you this: If I'm on trial in your court and you know I'm lying. To the quick of you, but you can't prove it then what do you do with me?

**Defence**    Then I let you go.

**Prosecution**    Which is pretty irrelevant if we're arguing over the existence or non-existence of my knowledge of the presence of my phone charger in my bag for example or whether I fancy a curry for my dinner or where I've put my car keys but what if we're arguing about the existence or non-existence of my knowledge of an act of massacre or terrorism or rape or cannibalism?

**Defence**    We're slow. We're methodical. We're rigorous. We're tireless in our attempts to build up concrete evidence. Without that evidence then we let you free.

**Prosecution**    We're utterly impotent.

**Defence**    We play by the rules.

**Prosecution**    We're morally redundant.

**Defence**    Because if we don't follow the ordinances of the Statute or the legislature of the courts we're working in then even if we win a case we lose it.

**Prosecution**    Always? Even if a case takes years and years? Even if an accused dies in court? Even if a pernickety determination to adhere to that conduct means that that same rapist, that same cannibal and I'm not talking metaphorically about cannibalism here by the way.

**Defence**    I know you're not.

**Prosecution**   That same cannibal goes free. He goes free and rapes and murders and eats again. And aborts babies with a penknife again. And throws children in a ditch again. Even then we adhere to the rules of conduct?

**Defence**   Absolutely.

**Prosecution**   Then what we're doing here is futile. It's moral masturbation. We're getting off on how fucking moral we are. We're not actually achieving anything or helping anybody.

*

**Ubu***'s cell.*

**Ubu, Jailor**.

**Ubu**   What's your name?

**Jailor**   Did you ask me a question?

**Ubu**   I did sir, yes. I'm sorry. I wanted to know what your name is.

**Jailor**   That's none of your fucking business.

**Ubu**   No. I know that. I'm sorry.

*There is some time.*

**Jailor**   I'm your fucking Jailor you stupid fuck.

**Ubu**   Yes.

**Jailor**   You don't ask me my name. My name is Jailor as far as you're concerned. That's it. Jailor.

**Ubu**   Yes.

**Jailor**   Or sir.

**Ubu**   Yes. Yes sir.

I'm sorry.

I just thought. We're going to be together for a long time.

**Jailor**  Don't think then.

**Ubu**  What?

**Jailor**  'Fucking what fucking sir?'

**Ubu**  Sorry sir, what sir?

**Jailor**  I fucking said 'Don't think then.'

**Ubu**  Right.

**Jailor**  Too many fucking people think around here.

**Ubu**  Yes.

**Jailor**  That's what fucking gets most of the fuckers into this fucking trouble in the first place.


*

*Courtroom.*

*Case for the Defence.*

**Defence, Prosecution, Judge, Major General-in-Chief, Registrar, Ubu.**

**Defence**  Major General-in-Chief what was the first you heard of Mr Ubu's plans to kill King Wenceslas?

**Major General-in-Chief**  He invited me to dinner. He got me on my own. He told me he wanted to speak to me. He ordered me to sit down. He told me he was going to make me the Major General-in-Chief. I was like 'How you gonna do that? You gonna kill the King or something?'

**Defence**  Just for the Court can you clarify that it was you who suggested to him that he might kill the King is that right?

**Major General-in-Chief**  No. He already had the idea.

**Defence**   But he didn't mention it. You mentioned it. Is that right?

**Major General-in-Chief**   He asked me if I'd be Major General-in-Chief.

**Defence**   And you suggested that one way he might implement his suggested plan for you is by killing the King is that right Major General?

**Major General-in-Chief**   Yes but –

**Defence**   Mr Ubu's first plan was to poison the king was it not?

**Major General-in-Chief**   I think it was, yes.

**Defence**   But the King wasn't poisoned was he?

**Major General-in-Chief**   No he was stabbed.

**Defence**   It was your plan to stab him wasn't it Major General?

**Major General-in-Chief**   It was a suggestion –

**Defence**   That you made with the words 'I suggest: one slash of the sabre, to slice him in pieces from head to toe.' Didn't you Major General?

**Major General-in-Chief**   I did yes.

**Defence**   It was also your suggestion that you 'pile on him, yelling and shouting!' taking care to 'scare off the guards'. Wasn't it Major General?

**Major General-in-Chief**   Yes it was.

**Defence**   And as we've seen already in this Court it was you and McClub who actually killed the King, not my client at all was it?

**Major General-in-Chief**   No. It was us who actually killed the King.

**Defence**   This is all your doing isn't it?

**Major General-in-Chief**    No.

**Defence**    In that the massacres in the FKB were motivated by wealth and that it was you who suggested to Mr Ubu ways of achieving this wealth it wouldn't be unreasonable to suggest that if Mr Ubu had never met you none of this would have happened, would it?

*The* **Major General-in-Chief** *is bewildered by the triple negative.*

**Major General-in-Chief**    No.

**Defence**    No. It wouldn't. Thank you.

**Major General-in-Chief**    He's sitting over there.

**Defence**    I'm sorry?

**Major General-in-Chief**    How am I meant to answer questions like that when he's there?

**Defence**    Major General?

**Major General-in-Chief**    You don't know what he could do to me.

**Judge**    Major General, I assure you that you are perfectly safe. Mr Ubu is powerless to move.

**Major General-in-Chief**    Look at him. He's sitting right there.

**Judge**    Major General please calm down.

**Major General-in-Chief**    He doesn't need to move. Some things don't happen on the outside. Everything I said I take it all back. He's right behind you. He's there. He's sitting there.

**Defence**    Major General why did you cross yourself? Just now you crossed yourself didn't you? Was that because you are aware that *you* are more guilty of the crimes my client is charged with than he is?

**Major General-in-Chief**   No. Ask him. He knows. He's there.

**Defence**   And when you deny your guilt you're lying aren't you?

**Major General-in-Chief**   No I am telling the truth and nothing but the truth.

**Defence**   I think you are telling anything but the truth.

No more questions Your Honour.

**Prosecution**   Whose idea was it to kill the bankers?

**Major General-in-Chief**   Mr Ubu's.

**Prosecution**   Whose idea was it to kill the judges?

**Major General-in-Chief**   Mr Ubu's.

**Prosecution**   Whose idea was it to kill the landed gentry?

**Major General-in-Chief**   Mr Ubu's.

**Prosecution**   And the tactic to suffocate these 1600 people in a closed mass grave whose idea was that?

**Major General-in-Chief**   Mr Ubu's.

*

*Courtroom.*

*The case for the Defence.*

**Defence, Prosecution, Judge, Ubu, Registrar**.

**Defence**   Whose idea was it to kill King Wenceslas?

**Ubu**   It was my wife's.

**Defence**   You tried to dissuade her didn't you?

**Ubu**   I did.

**Defence**   What did she do?

**Ubu**   She accused me of not being a man. She teased me. She threatened me.

**Defence**   You attempted to tell the King, to warn him didn't you?

**Ubu**   I did.

**Defence**   What stopped you?

**Ubu**   My wife. She begged me not to. She mocked me.

**Defence**   Whose idea was it to stab the King as opposed to poison him?

**Ubu**   The Major General-in-Chief's.

**Defence**   You deferred to him a lot on such matters didn't you?

**Ubu**   He knew much more about killing people than I did. I've never killed anybody.

**Defence**   Until that point?

**Ubu**   Or since. I've never actually killed anybody.

**Defence**   Mr Ubu, who killed the King?

**Ubu**   That was McClub. He stabbed him under his ribs.

**Defence**   Once you'd become King though, you were desperately greedy for more money weren't you?

**Ubu**   Only because I thought Ma would be cruel to me if I didn't keep getting her stuff.

**Defence**   Why did you kill the judges and the bankers and the gentry?

**Ubu**   I didn't kill them. I put them in prison. I had no idea what would happen to them. It's not like I built the prison. I'd never even used it before. The Major General-in-Chief had. He never told me what would happen. Nobody warned me. I thought it was funny. I was trying to make people happy.

**Defence**   You were trying to make people happy?

**Ubu**   I wanted to make my wife happy by buying her more things. I wanted to make people happy by making them laugh.

**Defence**   Who laughed when you did that?

**Ubu**   Everybody did.

**Defence**   No further questions Your Honour.

**Prosecution**   Why did you stamp on the King's foot?

**Ubu**   It was an accident.

**Prosecution**   What did you mean when you said to the Major General-in-Chief and his army 'It's time'?

**Ubu**   I don't remember saying that.

**Prosecution**   When you got the crown you told the Major General-in-Chief to 'See to the rest of them.' You meant for him to kill the Prince didn't you? So that you could retain power, didn't you Mr Ubu?

**Ubu**   No. I was nervous. I didn't want to get hurt. I was always nervous. I'm afraid I'm something of a coward.

**Prosecution**   When the Major General-in-Chief suggested sharing your wealth you said to him, and I quote from a sworn affidavit, 'I'm here to make my pile. Mine, every penny, mine.' What did you mean by that?

**Ubu**   I wanted to make money. I like money. Don't you? Doesn't everybody here? This whole world has been built upon the process of making and keeping money for the past five hundred years.

**Prosecution**   Ma Ubu begged you not to kill the gentry at the Christmas massacre didn't she?

**Ubu**    No. She said I was strict. She asked me to go easy. But she was laughing. Everybody was.

**Prosecution**    She begged you not to kill the judges didn't she?

**Ubu**    No. She said I was being fierce. But she said it like she was enjoying it.

**Prosecution**    She begged you not to kill the bankers too Mr Ubu didn't she?

**Ubu**    No. She told me I was a fine King.

**Prosecution**    Mr Ubu are you in any way ashamed of what you've done?

**Ubu**    I've not done anything.

**Prosecution**    Are you ashamed of killing Norbert Nurdle's family?

**Ubu**    That was my soldiers, not me.

**Prosecution**    Are you ashamed of robbing and torturing Achras?

**Ubu**    I never touched him.

What are these people doing?

*He gestures out to the audience.*

**Prosecution**    Which people?

**Ubu**    The people behind you.

**Prosecution**    That's none of your concern.

**Ubu**    What are they doing?

**Judge**    Mr Ubu please all that we need you to do is to answer the questions that are asked of you.

**Ubu**    What's she doing?

What's her job?

**Judge**   Mr Ubu I warn you that it is entirely within my powers to hold you in contempt of this Court and that the consequences of being held in contempt of this Court are severe for you and for your Defence Counsel.

**Ubu**   Don't I know you? I recognise your face from somewhere.

**Judge**   Mr Ubu, please will you answer the question that the Prosecution Counsel has asked you.

**Ubu**   Didn't we? Did we used to date one another or something like that? I have to say I hope not. You're very ugly.

**Judge**   Mr Ubu, please will you answer the question that the Prosecution Attorney has asked you.

**Ubu**   How long have I been here?

**Judge**   Mr Ubu?

**Ubu**   How long has this been going on? This trial? It feels like hours and hours.

**Judge**   Mr Ubu would you like a glass of water?

**Ubu**   I think I would please. How long has this been going on for?

**Judge**   Could you fetch Mr Ubu a glass of water please?

**Ubu**   Is that what she's here for? Is she here to fetch glasses of water?

**Judge**   Mr Ubu this is the 436th day of the trial.

**Ubu** *can't speak for a while*

**Ubu**   The 436th day?

**Judge**   That's right Mr Ubu.

**Ubu**   I've been here for 436 days?

**Judge**   In this Court. You've been in the Penal Institution since your arrest in Frankfurt am Main in March 2008.

**Ubu**    Oh.

*Everybody looks at him.*

Can I, do you mind if I sit down?

*He sits. Sips his water.*

It doesn't feel like 436 days. I feel a bit. I think I'm losing track of time a little bit.

\*

*Courtroom.*

**Ubu**'s *statement.*

**Judge, Ubu, Defence, Prosecution, Registrar.**

**Judge**    Mr Ubu. We are about to retire and consider our verdict. You have the right to make a statement to the Court. Is there anything further you wish to be taken into account before we do so?

**Ubu**    Thank you Your Honour. I have prepared a statement which with your permission I will present to the Court.

Your Honour, the tenets of this tribunal are built upon the Rome Statute of 2002 which is constructed in response to the Universal Declaration of Human Rights of 1948. Your Honour the Declaration is specious.

Not everybody is born free. Not everybody is born equal. Not everybody is born with reason. Not everybody is born with conscience. To pretend that they are is dishonest. The tenets on which the Declaration was signed are lies. The tenets on which this Court is built are lies. The tenets on which your organisation is built are lies.

It's important to you this isn't it?

**Judge**    I'm sorry?

**Ubu**   This. This trial. This language. This building. This tape recorder. It's important to you.

**Defence** *looks at* **Ubu**.

**Ubu**   You need it. You need a big building sitting on the edge of the city. You need it to be built with glass and concrete. You need it to tower like a football stadium.

**Judge**   I'm not sure I understand what you mean.

**Ubu**   Can I ask you, is the building this big to keep me inside or is it this big to show everybody how hard you're *trying* to keep me inside? Is the architecture for me or is it for all the people gathering outside the front gates? Or watching on the television? In their hotel rooms? On CNN? On Fox News? On BBC News 24?

**Judge**   The architecture is entirely functional.

**Ubu**   Do you know what is going on in my head as I stand hear listening to you talking about talking and about honour and about law and about justice and about the things that I have done? Spion Kop 1900. Guedecort 1916. Constantinople 1915. St Petersburg 1905. Munich 1923. Gijon 1936. Berlin 1938. Warsaw 1943. Tarawa 1943. Davao 1941. Belsen 1943. Nagasaki 1945. Dresden 1945. Algiers 1957. Saigon 1968. My Lai 1968. Biafra 1969. Phnom Penh 1975. Sharpeville 1960. Tehran 1988. Santiago 1990. Beirut 1983. Kabul 1980. Sarajevo 1992. Nyarubuye 1994. Grozny 2000. Port au Prince 2004. Omagh 1998. Manhattan Island 2001. Baghdad 2003. Gaza 2009.

Thank you Your Honour. I have completed my statement.

*

**Ubu**'s *cell*.

**Ubu**, **Jailor**.

**Ubu**   Sir. Excuse me sir.

**Jailor**   What?

**Ubu**   What time is it?

**Jailor**   What?

**Ubu**   Could you tell me what time it is sir, please?

**Jailor**   Quarter to five.

**Ubu**   Right. Quarter to five.

**Jailor**   Nearly ten to. Twelve minutes to, to be precise.

**Ubu**   Thank you.

Thank you sir.

How long do you think they'll be?

**Jailor**   Who?

**Ubu**   The judges?

**Jailor**   I have no fucking idea. It is fucking none of my business.

**Ubu**   No.

You're the last friendly face I'll ever see.

**Jailor**   You fucking what?

**Ubu**   Yours is the last friendly face I'll ever see.

**Jailor**   Well.

I'll tell you something for fucking nothing.

Nobody's ever said my face was friendly before. People normally tell me my face is ugly. I've got a cruel face, I always thought.

**Ubu**   Will you come and visit me when I get out?

You could come round to my house. You could bring your family. Bring your children. If the weather's nice I'll get the barbecue out. There's a lake near to where I live. If you brought your swimming things we could go for a swim in the lake and then have a barbecue.

Are they paying you lots of money?

**Jailor**   More than some people get paid. Not as much as others.

**Ubu**   You like a lot of money I bet don't you?

What do you think happens when you die?

**Jailor**   You won't die. They won't execute you. Not this lot. They'll keep you here.

**Ubu**   Here?

**Jailor**   Or in a box somewhere. You'll be in a glass box.

Your ankles will be in plastic cuffs.

You won't be able to speak. They'll put a gag on you probably.

**Ubu**   What do you think happens though?

**Jailor**   I think you just finish. There's no sound. There's no feeling. No smell. There's no taste. There's no colour. And no sense that there ever has been. Or will be. And no sense of that absence. There's no god. You don't miss your children. You don't know if they miss you.

**Ubu**   I won't miss my children anyway. I don't have any children. I won't miss anybody. I don't think anybody will miss me. I never thought they would.

I'm scared Ma.

**Jailor**   I'm not your fucking mother.

*He leaves.*

**Ubu**    I hate it in here.

I can't sleep at night.

And if I do I have the most awful dreams.

I dreamed one night that there was this field of horses and they went wild and they started fighting each other and they started chewing through each other's throats. One time I dreamt that the sky was full of stars but all of the stars started to bleed and burst. I dreamt that it was raining oil. I dreamt that all the metal in this place started crying. Ubu – watch the skies! Ubu – wake up! Ubu – this is what you did! This is what you have to do.

*As he talks he begins to rock.*

*His rocking becomes more violent.*

*He begins punching himself in the head.*

*He begins hitting his head on the floor and the walls of the prison.*

*He rubs his cock ferociously.*

*He pisses.*

*He starts laughing a bit.*

*He sings the melody of Beethoven's Ninth Symphony.*

*He starts gnashing his teeth.*

*He starts biting his own arms. His arms start bleeding.*

*He tries to bite through the inside of his own cheeks.*

*He sings 'God Save Our Gracious Me'.*

*Sudden black.*

# King Ubu

*A new version of* Ubu Roi *by Alfred Jarry*
*written by Simon Stephens*
*from a translation by Kenneth McLeish*

## Characters

**Pa Ubu**
**Ma Ubu**
**Dogpile**
**McClub**
**Good King Wenceslas**
**Prince Billiam in Skates**
**Nobs**
**Judges**
**Bankers**
**Norbert Nurdle**
**Achras**

*This version should be performed by puppets.*

**One**

**Pa Ubu** *alone*. **Ma Ubu** *enters*.

**Pa Ubu**   Ah shitters!

**Ma Ubu**   Watch your language Pa Ubu!

**Pa Ubu**   Shut your gob Ma! Or I'll bash your block off.

**Ma Ubu**   Not my block Pa, you nobster. Someone else's.

**Pa Ubu**   Bugger me backwards, what are you waffling on about?

**Ma Ubu**   Think about it Pa Ubu. Are you really happy with who you are?

**Pa Ubu**   Of course I am. Shitters! Who wouldn't be? Captain of the Guard, Eye and Ear of Good King Wenceslas, Past President of the Battalions of Baleshnik, Thane of Four-Door. What more could a blubbery bugger want?

**Ma Ubu**   Who gives a toss about the Thane of Four-Door? You want to get your block measured up for the crown of Baleshnik.

**Pa Ubu**   Ma Ubu, what are you on about?

**Ma Ubu**   Use your imagination you nobster! Good King Wenceslas! Off with his head!

**Pa Ubu**   Ma Ubu you worm bucket! I'm Captain of the Guard. Murder Good King Wenceslas? His Maj of Baleshnik? I'd rather die.

**Ma Ubu** (*aside*)   Shitters. (*Aloud*.) You want to be Daddy Mouse for ever? Poor Daddy Mouse?

**Pa Ubu**   Bugger me backwards you blubbery tit, I'd rather be poor, honest Daddy Mouse than Big Fat Cat that Nicked the Cream.

*He goes, slamming the door.*

**Ma Ubu** (*calling*)   If you were King you could have a great big hat! And a brolly! And a coat that trailed along the floor!

*She is left alone.*

Shitters, what a tight-arse. Never mind. Slibbady jibbet I'll nobble the nobster. With God's good help, not to mention mine, I'll be Queen of Baleshnik by Saturday.

**Pa Ubu** *comes back.*

**Pa Ubu** Did you say a great big hat?


**Two**

**Pa Ubu**, **Ma Ubu**.

**Pa Ubu**   Bugger me backwards, I'm starving. Ma Ubu, you look really ugly today. Is it because we've got company? Here they are. Captain Dogpile and his Barmpot McClub.

*The door opens.* **Dogpile** *enters. With* **McClub**.

**Dogpile**   Oi, Ma Ubu, what's for dinner?

**Ma Ubu**   Bull Bugger Soup. Calfcollops. Chicken. Pâté de Dog. Turkey bum. Ice cream, lettuce, apples, hotpot, tartyfarts, cauliflower shitter.

**Dogpile/McClub**   Munchmunchmunchmunchmunch munchmuchunchmunch.

**Pa Ubu**   Blubbery fat bum holes! I'm paying for this. What d'you take me for, a bank?

Out, out, you two. Captain Dogpile, I want a word.

**Ma Ubu/McClub**   Hey! We haven't finished.

**Pa Ubu**   Oh yes you have. Out, out! Dogpile, sit.

*No one moves.*

Here, Captain Dogpile, I'm going to make you Lord de Lawdy Major General-in-Chief.

**Dogpile**   Pardon, Pa Ubu? I thought you were skint.

**Pa Ubu**   In a day or two, with your help, I'll be King of Baleshnik.

**Dogpile**   You're going to kill Good King Wenceslas?

**Pa Ubu**   Aren't you a clever flucker! A flucking brainbox is you innit?

**Dogpile**   If you're doing for Good King Wenceslas, count me in. I'm his mortal enemy. Me and McClub.

**Pa Ubu** (*falling on his neck*)   Dogpile! My darling!


**Three**

*The royal palace.* **Pa Ubu**, **Ma Ubu**, **Dogpile**, **McClub**, *the* **King**.

*The* **King** *parades around being regal.*

**Pa Ubu**   OK, lads. Time to get this plot moving. Who's got an idea?

**Dogpile**   I suggest: one slash of the sabre, to slice him in snippets from snitch to shoe.

**McClub/Ma Ubu**   Yay! Our hero! Whee! Yeehah!

**Dogpile**   Hang on. We've got to scare off the other guards.

**Pa Ubu**   Got it! I stamp on his toe. He kicks me. I shout 'SHITTERS' – and that's the signal. You all pile in.

**Ma Ubu**   Then as soon as he's dead, you grab the crown.

**Dogpile**   And I and the lads sort out the rest of the twattle buckets.

**Pa Ubu**   Especially that shitter the Prince Billiam in Skates!

**Four**

*The parade ground.*

**King Wenceslas, Pa Ubu, Dogpile, McClub.**

**King**    Baron Ubu, stand beside one, you and your chaps.
It's time to inspect the troops.

*He peers out and examines the audience. His tiny son* **Prince
Billiam in Skates** *is with him.*

Prince Billiam. Look posh and have a bloody good gander.
That's the way to do it.

**Ubu***'s men gather around the* **King.**

**King**    Ah! The Forty-seventh Mounted Whores Lard
Parade. Isn't it something?

**Pa Ubu**    They're fat flucking blubbery bum holes!.

**King**    Pa Ubu, what's the matter with you today you
nobster?

**Pa Ubu**    This.

*He stamps on the* **King***'s foot.*

**Pa Ubu**    SHITTERS! It's time!

**Dogpile**    Pile on, lads.

*They all attack the* **King.** **McClub** *kills the* **King.**

**King**    You and all Ubu you bollock bucket! Bug Rit!
Billykins run! One's dead as a doughnut.

**Pa Ubu**    Shut yer hole yer pie face trollop. Right. Yew lot.
Snacker the rest of the shitters. Specially that Prince.

*There's a big fight. Everybody batters everybody else until* **Pa Ubu,
Ma Ubu, Dogpile** *are left alone.*

**Pa Ubu**    Bugger my blubbery bum hole, I'm the king. I've
had the party . . . got the 'angover . . . I'm here to make my

pile. Mine, every penny, mine. All I need now is the great big cloak.

**Ma Ubu**   Very naice, Pa Ubu. It's naice being royale.

**Pa Ubu**   Bring the nob-box, the nob-hook, the nob-knife, the nob-ledger – and the nobs.

*The* **Nobs** *are pushed forward, roughly.*

**Ma Ubu**   Pa Ubu, seel vooo play! Go easy. Don't do it! You've gone too far!

**Pa Ubu**   Shurrup Frenchie! S'my money! Royal decree. To enrich the state, I'm going to do in all the nobs and snitch their loot.

**Nobs**   Ooh! Aah! Help!

**Pa Ubu**   Come here, nobs. The lot of you. I'm not rich enough yet, so you're all for the chop. You've got it, you shitters, I need it. Open the door! Stuff the nobs down the tube.

*He opens the big wooden door. The* **Nobs** *are stuffed down the hatch.*

**Pa Ubu**   Get a nurdle on. I've laws to pass.

*The* **Judges** *shuffle on.*

**Pa Ubu**   Judges first, then bankers.

**Several Judges**   Objection! *Nolle prosequi. Status quo.*

**Pa Ubu**   Shurrup yer shitter! Law Number One: judges' salaries. Abolished.

**Judges**   What'll we live on? We're all skint.

**Pa Ubu**   Live on the fines.

**First Judge**   Impossible.

**Second Judge**   Outrageous.

**Judges**   Under these conditions, we refuse to judge.

**Pa Ubu**    All judges down the tube!

*They struggle, in vain.* **Pa Ubu** *opens the door. The* **Judges** *are pushed down the tube.*

*The* **Bankers** *shuffle on.*

**Ma Ubu**    What're you doing, Pa Ubu? Who'll do the judging, now?

**Pa Ubu**    Watch and see. Who's next, now? Bankers. First off, I want half of all charges.

**Bankers**    You're joking.

**Pa Ubu**    And here are some charges: property, 10 per cent, commerce and industry, 25 per cent, marriage and death fifty nicker each.

**First Banker**    Pa Ubu, it just isn't viable.

**Pa Ubu**    Take the piss, would you, you shitter? Down the tube!

*The* **Bankers** *are downchuted.*

**Ma Ubu**    Fine king you are, Ubu, mon sewer, killing the whole world. Tray benny!

**Pa Ubu**    Don't worry, girl. I'll go from town to town, collect the cash first.

*He leers out and addresses the audience.*

Right. You nobholes. Who's the oldest out of you lot?

**Norbert Nurdle** *steps forward from behind him.*

**Norbert Nurdle**    Eye yam. Moi name is Norbert Nurdle. This is moi woife. Nora Nurdle.

**Pa Ubu**    Right. Listen. Num Bum Nuffle Shuckit. D'you want these frensomine to clip your clackers?

**Norbert Nurdle**    But Your Majesty hasn't said anything.

**Pa Ubu**    Wrong, pal. I've been flapping my gob for
the whole last hour. Fetch out your tax-pot, now, or die.
Cashandlers: the cashcart!

*The cashcart is brought in.*

**Norbert Nurdle**    We paid in full, the Feast of St Multiple
Ult.

**Pa Ubu**    So what? I've changed the rules. It was in the
paper: all taxes to be paid twice over, except those I may
dream up later, to be paid three times. Simple, innit? I make
my fortune, snickersnack, then kill the whole world and
buggeroff. I am the bloody king. Dogpile. Do your dirty do.

**Dogpile** *kills* **Norbert Nurdle**'s *wife.*

**Norbert Nurdle**    My wife! You scoundrels! I'm off!

**Dogpile** *runs off after him.*

**Ma Ubu**    Dogpile! Don't go! Mon armour!

**Pa Ubu**    Shut yer blubber, bum shitter. We don't need him
anyway!

**Ma Ubu**    Bad idea, Pa Ubu. He may turn nasty.

**Pa Ubu**    I'm so frightened!

**Ma Ubu**    Pa Ubu, be careful. He's got justice fighting on his
side.

**Pa Ubu**    So bloody what? We've got injustice, haven't we?
You piss me off, Ma Ubu.

**Ma Ubu**    Look. See! We got a postcard. 'Having a lovely
taime. Tsar Alexis of all the Russkies really naice. Invading
tomorrow to put Wenceslas's Child back on throne and stuff
your guts. Regards Dogpile.'

**Pa Ubu**    I'm done for. The naughty man's coming to hurt
me. St Nickerless, oelpme, I'll give you all my taxes. God, tell
me what to do. I'll even pray. Oh what am I to do?

*He sobs and sobs.*

**Ma Ubu**   Pa Ubu, there's only one thing for it. War.

**McClub**   Fight! Fight! Fight! Fight! Fight!

**Pa Ubu**   Oh brilliant. Thrashed again. Ma Ubu, give me my breastplate. My poky-stick. I'll be so loaded, I won't be able to run if they're after me.

**Ma Ubu**   Coward.

**Pa Ubu**   This blubbery bastard shickastick!. This nobster nobhook. They won't stay put. I'll never be ready. The Russkies'll come and kill me.

Never mind. I'm off. To war. I'll kill the whole world. Especially those who don't march in step. Ubu be angry, Ubu pullout oo teef, oo tongue.

**Ma Ubu**   Pa Ubu, tata. Give that Tsar whatfor.

**Pa Ubu**   Watch me. I'm a nose-knotting, teeth-twisting, tongue-tearing, shitter!


**Five**

**Ubu, Achras, McClub.**

**Pa Ubu**   Bugger me blubber belly, mate, this placeayours is rubbish. I was ringin that bell for an hour. An when they did open the door, it was so small my gurdlenacker nearly knotted itself gettin through.

**Achras**   Sorry, sir. We don't get visitors your size. If I'd known, I'd have got a bigger door. You'll have to excuse me. Absent-minded old professor. Snark. Expert in the field.

**Pa Ubu**   Oojoo think you are? There's only one mindere, that's mine. Still, nehmind. I've decided to bless your umbleome. It suits us. We're movin in.

**Achras**   I'm sorry, sir . . .

**Pa Ubu**   You're afraid you'll be in the way. Don't worry, if you are we'll tell you. Now, I want to see the kitchen, the dining room. You'll find two trunks outside the door. Bring the buggers in! You mardy mumbling mutterer.

**Achras**   Taking over someone else's house. It's, it's unbelievable.

**Pa Ubu**   A lilbird's just tole me, Ma Ubu my ballanchain's been avinitoff with some blubbering nobster. 'E's mine. I'll avim. Stagger me sideways, 'e woneven know wot itim.

**Achras**   That's very sad. Having it off with your wife. How sad.

**Pa Ubu**   Sad for im. What'm I plannin forim? McClub! Stake up the bum.

**Achras**   Ah. Yes. I don't quite see . . . Where do I come in?

**Pa Ubu**   Stagger me sideways, I aveto practise.

**Achras**   Ah. Sir. No, I'm sorry. I won't. I simply won't. You nick my house, you throw me out, and now you want to kill me. It's ridiculous. It's surreal.

*The stake begins to rise beneath his chair.*

It's unheard of . . . I'm an old man . . . A man of science . . . What're you doing? It isn't fair.

*He faints. The stake is driven up his arse.*

**McClub**   Pa Ubu, look. Dogpile and his Wusskies.

**Pa Ubu**   Noodlenackerin, teethtwistin, earnottin bumsnickin, bone-grindin, marrowsuckin, thassall we can do forem.

**McClub**   Yeehah, Pa Ubu, yay!

**Pa Ubu**   God save our gracious me, Long live our noble me, Pour me some pee! I love it. I love you all.

*A Russkie cannonball flies in and smashes the stage apart leaving* **Pa Ubu** *alone on stage.*

One's poky-stick did sterling work. One would have completely done them all in if dire, sudden dread hadn't drained one's deadliness. One was unexpectedly compelled to do a runner. You want to be like me. Lion-hearted, but cautious. I massacred four of them, in person, if you count the ones that were dead already when I did 'em. Behold, as the flowers of the field are felled, hoed by the heedless, heartless hoe of the heedless, heartless hoer who heartlessly hacks their heads. Bloody good speech. Why thangyew. Pity no one else was listening.

It's getting late. Time for bed.